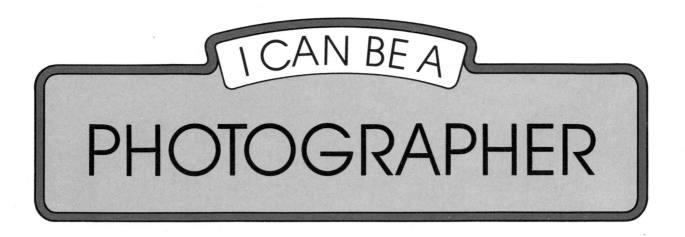

I CAN BE A
PHOTOGRAPHER

By Christine Osinski

Prepared under the direction of Robert Hillerich, Ph.D.

 CHILDRENS PRESS ®

CHICAGO

Library of Congress Cataloging in Publication Data

Osinski, Christine.
  I can be a photographer.

  Includes index.
  Summary: A brief introduction to the work of
photographers.
  1. Photography—Vocational guidance—Juvenile literature.
[1. Photography. 2. Photographers. 3. Occupations] I. Title.
TR154.085 1986   770'.23'2   85-30854
ISBN 0-516-01894-9

Copyright ©1986 by Regensteiner Publishing Enterprises, Inc.
All rights reserved. Published simultaneously in Canada.
Printed in the United States of America.
1 2 3 4 5 6 7 8 9 10 R 95 94 93 92 91 90 89 88 87 86

PICTURE DICTIONARY

light meter

film

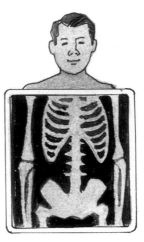

X ray

camera

shutter

lens

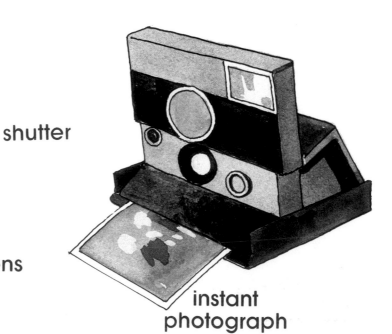

instant
photograph

chemicals print enlarger

darkroom

family portrait

family album

flash or strobe

still life

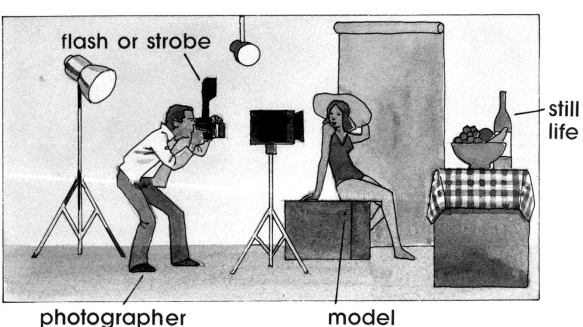

photographer model

studio

Photographs help us remember what our world was like at special times in our lives.

It is hard to imagine a world without photographs. Think of all the places you find photographs—in your school books, in newspapers and magazines, in your home. Photographs are everywhere.

must learn many things about how cameras work.

The lens is the eye of the camera. The shutter is its eyelid. When the shutter "blinks" open, it lets in light. Then the lens can see the subject being photographed. When the lens is focused properly, the picture will be sharp and clear.

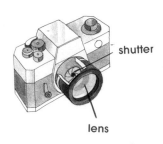

shutter

lens

Left: A hand-held light meter. Right: A camera with its lens detached

Most photographers
use light meters. Light
meters measure the
brightness of the light
around the subject. The
light meter tells the
camera how much light
to let in for the picture

light meter

film

darkroom

to come out well. Light bounces off the subject and goes into the camera. The light exposes the film, or creates an image of the subject on the film.

After the film is exposed to light, it is developed in a darkened room called a darkroom. The

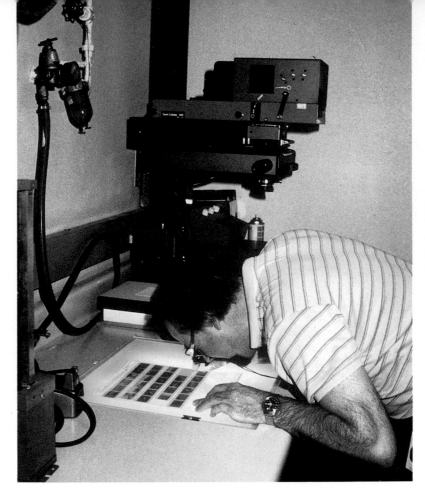

This photographer has developed his film. Now he is deciding which pictures to enlarge and print.

darkroom has a special yellow light that will not expose film.

Chemicals are used to develop the film. Once it is developed, prints are made. A

The enlarger (left) projects the small, film-sized image onto a large sheet of photographic paper. As the paper sits in a chemical bath (right), the picture gradually appears. It must be removed from the bath at just the right time. If left in, the picture would keep developing until it was totally black.

chemicals print enlarger

machine called an enlarger makes big prints from the film. Chemicals develop the print and the photograph appears!

Some cameras produce instant photographs. There is no need for a darkroom with these cameras. The picture appears right before your eyes!

instant photograph

Miami beats Florida State, 35-27.

Someone once said
that a picture is worth a
thousand words.
Sometimes a
photograph is better
than just words.

Photography brings
the world into your
home. When you read

words in a newspaper
or magazine, you also
look at pictures.

Photographers may
be sent to distant lands
to take pictures. These
photographs teach us
about people in other
countries.

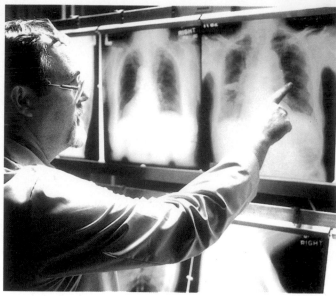

Left: An astronaut took this picture in outer space.
Right: An X ray is a picture of "inner space."

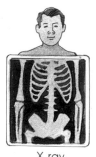

X ray

Photographs can be made in outer space and in the inside of your body. An X ray is a special kind of photograph that helps a doctor see inside the human body. These photographs show us what our eyes alone cannot see.

Have you ever gone to a portrait studio to have your family portrait or your graduation picture taken?

studio

Photographers who work in studios are called studio photographers. Studio photographers use special lights. Some are

family portrait

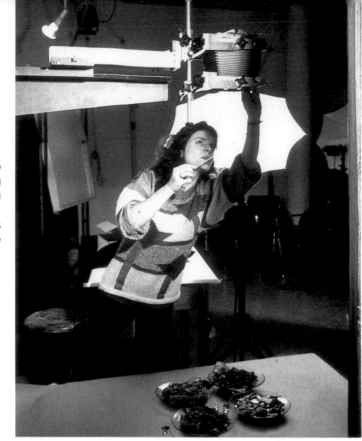

A studio photographer getting ready to take a picture of some food. Special umbrellas are used to shine light on the subject.

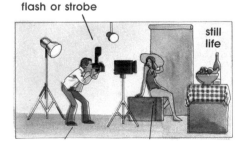

flash or strobe

still life

photographer   model

very bright. Others flash when the picture is taken. These are called flashes or strobes.

Sometimes models are photographed in a studio. "Still lifes" are photographed in a

These still lifes will be used as advertisements.

studio, too. A still life is an arrangement of nonliving objects, such as food or furniture. Often, these photographs are used in magazines.

Photographers must work in all kinds of weather. They may be called to many different places to take pictures, at night or in the day. Some photograph sports events, others photograph at parties.

Photographers at the Indianapolis 500 races (above) and at the Air Force Academy graduation (below)

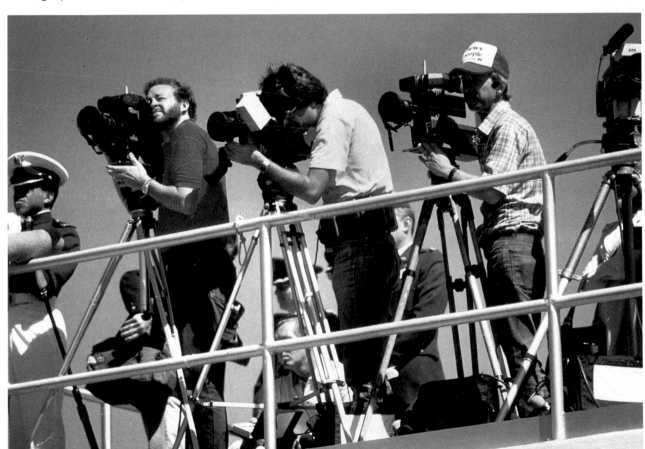

Perhaps you have had your picture taken by a professional photographer in school. Perhaps your mother or father has taken your picture at home on special holidays. We all like to have our pictures taken.

Some only photograph weddings. Others specialize in portraits. A photographer may work a whole day or an entire week to get just one good photograph!

Some photographs are as beautiful as paintings. Art museums collect these photographs and display them.

Perhaps you have had your picture taken by a professional photographer in school. Perhaps your mother or father has taken your picture at home on special holidays. We all like to have our pictures taken.

Photographers at the Indianapolis 500 races (above) and at the Air Force Academy graduation (below)

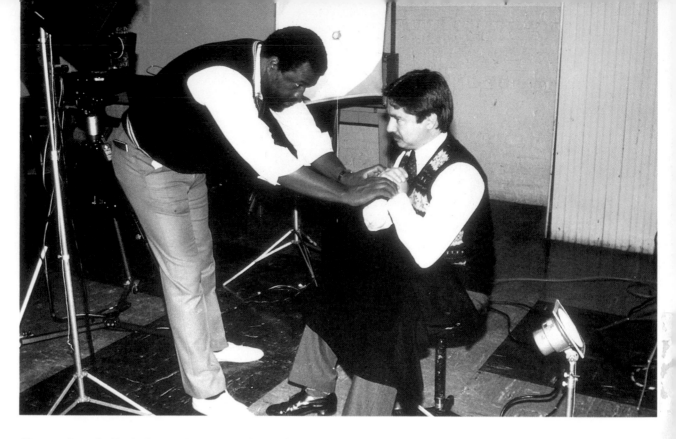

Above: A portrait photographer in his studio. Below: With a telephoto lens, a photographer can take a close-up picture of faraway objects.

Photographers record special times in our lives
that we will want to remember later.

It's fun to collect photographs. Some people put their photographs in family albums. Photographs show us what our parents looked like when they were young.

family album

When we grow up we
will want to remember
how we were as
children. Photographs
help us remember.

So, you can see how important photographs are. Photographers work very hard at what they do, but they also have fun. Would you like to take pictures of people and events that are important to you? Perhaps you will be a professional photographer!

WORDS YOU SHOULD KNOW

album (AL • bum)—a book with blank pages for collecting photographs

camera (KAM • er • uh)—a lightproof box used for taking pictures

chemicals (KEM • ih • kulz)—special substances used to develop photographic film and prints

darkroom (DARK • room)—a room in which film is processed. The room is dark except for a safelight, a light that will not expose light-sensitive film or paper.

develop (dih • VEL • up)—to treat film with chemicals to make an image appear on the film

enlarger (in • LAR • jer)—a piece of darkroom equipment used to make larger prints from smaller film

expose (ex • POZE)—to let light fall on light-sensitive film and create an image on it

film (FILM)—a strip or sheet of material that is sensitive to light

flash (FLASH)—a device that produces a short burst of light to light up something being photographed

focus (FOH • kus)—to adjust the lens of a camera so that the picture will be sharp and clear

lens (LENZ)—part of a camera through which light enters to expose the film

light meter (LITE MEET • er)—a small device for measuring the brightness of light around a subject. Some light meters are attached to a camera, and some are held separately.

model (MAHD • el)—a person who is photographed, for example, for an advertising photograph

portrait (PORE • tret)—a formal picture of a person or a group, usually taken to record a special occasion, time of life, or event

print (PRINT)—a copy of a picture made onto paper from developed film

shutter (SHUT • er)—part of a camera that opens and shuts quickly to let in light

still life (STIL LIFE)—a picture of nonliving objects, or still objects

strobe (STROHB)—a light that flashes to light up something being photographed

studio (STOO • dee • oh)—the workplace of a photographer or artist

X ray (EX RAY)—a picture taken with short-wave radiation instead of with light

INDEX

PHOTO CREDITS

Image Finders:
  © R. Flanagan—4, 22 (top), 25 (top)
  © C. Osinski—9 (right)

Journalism Services:
  © Paul F. Gero—25 (bottom)
  © Joseph Jacobson—Cover
  © Tom Pierson—27
  © Bruce Schulman—22 (bottom), 28
  © P. Tvarkunas—21 (top)
  © Scott Wanner—16 (right)

Courtesy National Aeronautics and Space Administration—16 (left)

Nawrocki Stock Photo:
  © Jeff Apoian—11, 12 (left), 19 (right)
  © Ted Cordingley—15
  © Robert M. Lightfoot—6 (right)
  © W. S. Nawrocki—26 (left)
  © Carlos Vergara—6 (left), 21 (bottom)

© C. Osinski—9 (left), 12 (right), 13, 14, 18, 26 (right)

© J. Savio—19 (left)

ABOUT THE AUTHOR

Christine Osinski has exhibited her photographs internationally. She currently teaches photography at the Cooper Union in New York City.